EVERYMAN,
I WILL GO WITH THEE
AND BE THY GUIDE,
IN THY MOST NEED
TO GO BY THY SIDE

EVERYMAN'S LIBRARY
POCKET POETS

LITTLE POEMS

❖❖❖❖❖❖❖❖❖❖

EDITED BY
MICHAEL HENNESSY

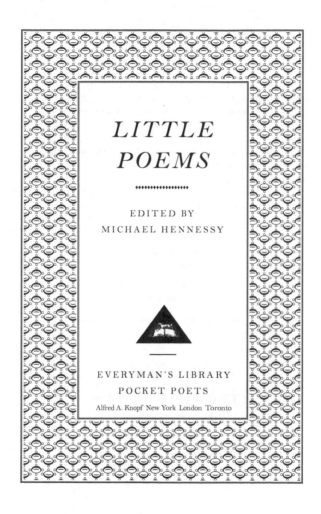

EVERYMAN'S LIBRARY
POCKET POETS

Alfred A. Knopf   New York   London   Toronto

THIS IS A BORZOI BOOK
PUBLISHED BY ALFRED A. KNOPF

This selection by Michael Hennessy
first published in Everyman's Library, 2023
Copyright © 2023 by Everyman's Library

Second printing (US)

everymanslibrary.com
www.everymanslibrary.co.uk

ISBN 978-0-593-53630-8 (US)
978-1-84159-828-4 (UK)

A CIP catalogue record for this book is available
from the British Library

Typography by Peter B. Willberg

Typeset in the UK by Input Data Services Ltd,
Isle Abbotts, Somerset

Printed and bound in Germany
by GGP Media GmbH, Pössneck

CONTENTS

MEDIEVAL AND EARLY MODERN POETS

SEVENTEENTH- AND EIGHTEENTH-CENTURY POETS

MODERN POETS: EARLY TWENTIETH
    CENTURY

MODERN POETS: MID-TWENTIETH CENTURY

CONTEMPORARY POETS

FOREWORD

Most of us experience literature for the first time in the form of a "little poem." Long before we've tasted our first solid food, we've heard a soothing lullaby spoken or sung by a parent, and before we start school, we have already begun to accumulate a storehouse of nursery rhymes. The sounds and rhythms of those little poems are embedded in memory, and we pass them down to the next generation.

But little poems range far beyond the nursery. Nearly all poets in all ages have written them. Even John Milton, author of the epic-length *Paradise Lost*, wrote a poem ten lines long. Milton's contemporary Robert Herrick, on the other hand, created many little poems, making them his signature genre. The same holds true for poets across time: those who favored longer forms occasionally wrote brief songs. And others – ancient Greek epigram writers, Japanese haiku poets, and modern writers like William Carlos Williams, Langston Hughes, and Dorothy Parker – often favored brevity.

What exactly qualifies as a "little poem"? There is no consensus, but the Italian word "sonetto," source of the English word "sonnet," means "little song," suggesting that fourteen lines may be a rule of thumb. But in this book, even a sonnet would be "long." All the poems

I have included – almost 300 of them, by more than 175 different authors – are under fourteen lines. Most range from two lines to twelve. A few have thirteen lines – just shy of a sonnet. Poets have been writing such poems for thousands of years, starting in the ancient world and continuing to the present day. The earliest work in this book is by the Greek poet Sappho, who lived in the seventh century BCE; the most recent is by poets still active in the 2020s, such as Carol Ann Duffy, Danez Smith, and Ocean Vuong.

What do little poems have in common besides their brevity? Probably not a great deal – except for their astonishing variety. Many are highly accessible on first reading, almost tweet-like. Others invite contemplation: they call us back to reread and ponder their lines. Despite their brevity, however, little poems can do most of what longer poems can do: tell a story; paint a picture; evoke an emotion; argue a point; make us laugh or cry. They can be serious or sarcastic, somber or silly, disturbing or comforting. And like all poems, they invite us to see the world with new eyes and to hear it with new ears.

The poems in this book do all those things. And their chronological arrangement highlights their diversity in surprising ways. The first section, for example, includes a mournful poem by first-century BCE Chinese Emperor Wu-ti about the death of his beloved mistress. But this poem stands in close proximity to two others by the Roman poet Martial making fun of people with bad hairpieces. Other sections likewise include juxtapositions that I hope will broaden conceptions of what poetry is and what it can do.

In the second section, works by Chaucer and Shakespeare inhabit the same space as the earliest written English version of the well-known children's mnemonic "Thirty Days Has November." And at the end of the section, readers will find a Thomas Dekker poem that Paul McCartney adapted 370 years later for the Beatles song "Golden Slumbers." The next section, too, contains many "serious" poems by such major seventeenth- and eighteenth-century figures as Bashō, Goethe, and Blake, but the section also offers lighter fare: Mother Goose nursery rhymes, a sharp-tongued political epigram by John Wilmot, Earl of Rochester, and two verses for fruit-sellers by Jonathan Swift. Likewise, the selection of nineteenth-century writing includes moving love poems by Alexander Pushkin and John Keats, but these classic pieces share space with a page of limericks and Emily Dickinson's playfully profound "I'm Nobody."

Modern and contemporary poets, who are amply represented in the final three sections of the book, demonstrate even more vividly the large arena that little poems occupy. Powerful poems about love are matched by comic poems on the same topic by contemporary British poet Wendy Cope. There is also a touching lullaby by Rudyard Kipling; a poem by W. H. Auden about the 1968 Soviet invasion of Czechoslovakia; a word-play rhyme by Shel Silverstein; and haiku by Masaoka Shiki, Richard Wright, and Jack Kerouac.

My hope is that readers will find this eclectic mix of little poems as rewarding to read as it was for me to assemble.

I wish to thank several people who have helped me along the way: Suparno Banarjee, Tom Grimes, Jane Holloway, Dan Lochman, Tomás Morín, Marilynn Olson, Cecily Parks, Diana Secker Tesdell, Nancy Tilka, Frédéric Trincot, and especially Nancy Grayson. The book would not exist without the love and support of Susie Tilka.

Michael Hennessy

LITTLE POEMS

A BLANK WHITE PAGE

is a meadow
after a snowfall
that a poem
hopes to cross

FRANCISCO X. ALARCÓN (1954–2016)

EARLY POETS
OF GREECE, ROME,
AND CHINA

ON POETRY

Like the bee, she consorts
  to concoct her dream
of a scented, pollen-yellow honey.

SIMONIDES (6TH CENTURY BCE)
TRANSLATED BY SHEROD SANTOS

BE KIND TO ME

Gongyla; I ask only
that you wear the cream
white dress when you come

Desire darts about your
loveliness, drawn down in
circling flight at sight of it

and I am glad, although
once I too quarrelled
with Aphrodite
                 to whom
I pray that you will
come soon

SAPPHO (7TH CENTURY BCE)
TRANSLATED BY MARY BARNARD

IT'S NO USE

Mother dear, I
can't finish my
weaving
          You may
blame Aphrodite

soft as she is

she has almost
killed me with
love for that boy

TONIGHT I'VE WATCHED

The moon and then
the Pleiades
go down

The night is now
half-gone; youth
goes; I am

in bed alone

YOU MAY FORGET BUT

Let me tell you
this: someone in
some future time
will think of us

WREATH

Though my aged head be grey,
And thy youth more fresh than May,
Fly me not; oh! rather see
In this wreath how gracefully
Roses with pale lilies join:
Learn of them, so let us twine.

ON DRINKING

Fruitful earth drinks up the rain,
Trees from earth drink that again,
The sea drinks the air, the sun
Drinks the sea, and him the moon:
Is it reason then d'ye think
I should thirst when all else drink?

ADONIS IN THE UNDERWORLD

Of all the pleasures in the upper world,
   what I miss most is sunlight,
after that the stars, a full moon, summer's
   late season harvest of fruits,
cucumber, apple, pomegranate, pear.

TRANSLATED BY SHEROD SANTOS

SEEK LOVE AMONG THE BRAVE

Learn, my friend, the lesson of Admetus,
whose fearless wife died in his stead:
seek love among the brave,
and shun the thankless coward.

TRANSLATION ADAPTED FROM J. M. EDMONDS

THE COCK SHALL CROW NO MORE

Never more with flapping wing
Shalt thou rouse me from my bed
As the dawn is reddening.
   Tyrant, thou art dead.
Lo the fox with stealthy bite
Slew thee as thou slept this night.

ELM TREE

Come stranger, come beneath this elm
   Where breezes soft caress;
And let the green of whispering leaves
   Assuage your weariness.
Drink to your fill of my cool fount,
   So fresh to wayworn feet,
And in the pleasure of my shade
   Forget the burning heat.

30   ANYTE (3RD CENTURY BCE)
TRANSLATED BY F. A. WRIGHT

POEM 70

Lesbia says she'd rather marry me
than anyone,
        though Jupiter himself came asking
or so she says,
        but what a woman tells her lover in desire
should be written out on air & running water.

POEM 85

I hate and I love. And if you ask me how,
I do not know: I only feel it, and I'm torn in two.

CATULLUS (*c.* 84–*c.* 54 BCE)
TRANSLATED BY PETER WHIGHAM

POEM 92

Lesbia for ever on me rails,
To talk of me she never fails.
Now, hang me, but for all her art,
I find that I have gain'd her heart.
My proof is this; I plainly see,
The case is just the same with me;
I curse her ev'ry hour sincerely,
Yet, hang me, but I love her dearly.

TRANSLATED BY JONATHAN SWIFT

POEM 101

Journeying over many seas & through many countries
I come dear brother to this pitiful leave-taking
the last gestures by your graveside
the futility of words over your quiet ashes.
Life cleft us from each other
pointlessly depriving brother of brother.
Accept then, in our parents' custom
these offerings, this leave-taking
echoing for ever, brother, through a brother's tears.
                                    – "Hail & Farewell".

CATULLUS (*c.* 84–*c.* 54 BCE)   33
TRANSLATED BY PETER WHIGHAM

MEETING IN THE ROAD

In a narrow road where there was not room to pass,
My carriage met the carriage of a young man.
And while his axle was touching my axle
In the narrow road, I asked him where he lived.
"The place where I live is easy enough to find,
Easy to find and difficult to forget.
The gates of my house are built of yellow gold;
The hall of my house is paved with white jade;
On the hall table flagons of wine are set.
I had summoned to serve me dancers of Han-tan.
In the midst of the courtyard grows a cassia-tree –
And candles on its branches flaring away in the night."

ON THE DEATH OF LI FU-JĒN

The sound of her silk skirt has stopped.
On the marble pavement dust grows.
Her empty room is cold and still.
Fallen leaves are piled against the doors.
       Longing for that lovely lady
How can I bring my aching heart to rest?

EMPEROR WU-TI (177–87 BCE)   35
TRANSLATED BY ARTHUR WALEY

EPIGRAM 10.47

Things that can bless a life and please,
   Sweetest Martial, they are these:
A store well left, not gain'd with toil,
   A house thine own and pleasant soil,
No strife, small state, a mind at peace,
   Free strength, and limbs free from disease,
Wise innocent friends, like and good,
   Unarted meat, kind neighbourhood,
No Drunken rest, from cares yet free,
   No sadd'ning spouse, yet chaste to thee,
Sleeps, that long Nights abbreviate,
   Because 'tis likening thy wish'd state,
Nor fear'd, nor joy'd at Death or Fate.

MARTIAL (*c.* 40–*c.* 104)
   TRANSLATED BY ABRAHAM COWLEY

EPIGRAM 10.61

Underneath this greedy stone,
Lies little sweet Erotion;
Whom the fates, with hearts as cold,
Nipt away at six years old.
Thou, whoever thou mayst be,
That hast this small field after me,
Let the yearly rites be paid
To her little slender shade;
So shall no disease or jar
Hurt thy house, or chill thy Lar;
But this tomb here be alone,
The only melancholy stone.

MARTIAL (*c.* 40–*c.* 104)
TRANSLATED BY LEIGH HUNT

EPIGRAM 5.9

A slight cold or a touch of flu,
but when THE SPECIALIST and all his crew
of a hundred students once are through,
and every inch of me's been handled twice
by a hundred medics' hands as cold as ice,
the pneumonia I didn't have I DO!

TRANSLATED BY TONY HARRISON

EPIGRAM 9.33

Outside the Baths you hear applause –
Flaccus, you know the likely cause.
Connoisseurs love fine workmanship,
Maron has let his towel slip.

TRANSLATED BY PETER PORTER

EPIGRAM 6.12

The golden hair that Galla wears
    Is hers: who would have thought it?
She swears 'tis hers, and true she swears,
    For I know where she bought it.

TRANSLATED BY SIR JOHN HARINGTON

EPIGRAM 6.57

With fictive locks and scented glue
    You hide your dome: who's fooling who?
A haircut? That's a simple matter.
    No clippers, please; just soap and water.

TRANSLATED BY DUDLEY FITTS

A GARDENER

Pomegranate yellow-coated, wrinkled fig,
    A purple cluster of new-gathered grapes,
A scented apple dewy from the twig,
    A filbert from its sheath of green that gapes,
A downy melon, bedded on the ground,
    A plum, an olive with its cloth of gold: –
These for the god hath planter Lamon found,
    And prays good health in tree and limb may hold.

PLUCKING THE RUSHES

A boy and girl are sent to gather rushes for thatching

Green rushes with red shoots,
Long leaves bending to the wind –
You and I in the same boat
Plucking rushes at the Five Lakes.
We started at dawn from the orchid-island:
We rested under the elms till noon.
You and I plucking rushes
Had not plucked a handful when night came!

TWO EPIGRAMS

I kept singing this, and I will call it out from the
    grave:
  "Drink, before you put on these clothes of dust."

Anastasia, the Graces blossom and you were their
    flower,
  and in your time the marriage bed
and before your time the grave held you. Father
  and husband weep for you bitterly. Even the
    boatman
of the dead weeps over you, not a whole year
  with your husband: sixteen and buried.

42   JULIAN THE EGYPTIAN (5TH CENTURY CE)
   TRANSLATED BY W. S. MERWIN

THOUGHTS IN THE SILENT NIGHT

Beside my bed a pool of light –
Is it hoarfrost on the ground?
I lift my eyes and see the moon,
I bend my head and think of home.

TRANSLATED BY YANG XIANYI AND GLADYS YANG

TAKING LEAVE OF A FRIEND

Blue mountains to the north of the walls,
White river winding about them;
Here we must make separation
And go out through a thousand miles of dead grass.

Mind like a floating wide cloud.
Sunset like the parting of old acquaintances
Who bow over their clasped hands at a distance.
Our horses neigh to each other
        as we are departing.

TRANSLATED BY EZRA POUND

DEER ENCLOSURE

On the empty mountain there is no one to be seen;
You only hear the echo of people talking.
The sun's returning rays enter the deep woods
And shine again on the dark green moss.

THINKING OF MY BROTHERS EAST OF THE MOUNTAINS ON THE FESTIVAL OF THE NINTH DAY OF THE NINTH MONTH, WHEN SEVENTEEN YEARS OLD

Here I am alone, a stranger
    in a strange land.
Whenever there's a festival
    I miss my family twice over.
Even from here I know my brothers
    will climb to a high place,
All decked out with sprays of dogwood –
    and with one person missing.

TRANSLATED BY PETER HARRIS

TRAVELLING NORTHWARD

Screech owls moan in the yellowing
Mulberry trees. Field mice scurry,
Preparing their holes for winter.
Midnight, we cross an old battlefield.
The moonlight shines cold on white bones.

SUNSET

Sunset glitters on the beads
Of the curtains. Spring flowers
Bloom in the valley. The gardens
Along the river are filled
With perfume. Smoke of cooking
Fires drifts over the slow barges.
Sparrows hop and tumble in
The branches. Whirling insects
Swarm in the air. Who discovered
That one cup of thick wine
Will dispel a thousand cares?

DU FU (712−70)   45
TRANSLATED BY KENNETH REXROTH

SPRING GRASSES

Long and heavy, the grasses on the plains –
Once in a year they wither and then they flourish.
The prairie fires do not burn them away
And when the spring wind blows they grow again.
Their distant scent encroaches on the old highway,
Their brilliant green reaches the deserted city walls.
As I see my noble friend on his way once more
Their abundance fills my heart as I say farewell.

BAI JUYI (772–846)
TRANSLATED BY PETER HARRIS

MEDIEVAL AND EARLY MODERN POETS

Not marble nor the gilded monuments
Of princes shall outlive this powerful rhyme,
But you shall shine more bright in these contents
Than unswept stone besmeared with sluttish time.

WILLIAM SHAKESPEARE (1564–1616)

From THE TRIADS OF IRELAND

Three slender things that best support the world:
the slender stream of milk from the cow's dug into
    the pail,
the slender blade of green corn upon the ground,
the slender thread over the hand of a skilled woman.

THE VIKING TERROR

Bitter is the wind tonight,
It tosses the ocean's white hair:
Tonight I fear not the fierce warriors of Norway
Coursing on the Irish Sea.

ANONYMOUS (9TH CENTURY)   49
TRANSLATED BY KUNO MEYER

TWO SONGS OF COLD MOUNTAIN

Born thirty years ago
I've traveled countless miles
along rivers where the green rushes swayed
to the frontier where the red dust swirled
I've made elixirs and tried to become immortal
I've read the classics and written odes
and now I've retired to Cold Mountain
to lie in a stream and wash out my ears

Who takes the Cold Mountain Road
takes a road that never ends
the rivers are long and piled with rocks
the streams are wide and choked with grass
it's not the rain that makes the moss slick
and it's not the wind that makes the pines moan
who can get past the tangles of the world
and sit with me in the clouds

50   HAN-SHAN (*fl.* 9TH CENTURY)
    TRANSLATED BY RED PINE

EVENING IN THE VILLAGE

Here in the mountain village
Evening falls peacefully.
Half tipsy, I lounge in the
Doorway. The moon shines in the
Twilit sky. The breeze is so
Gentle the water is hardly
Ruffled. I have escaped from
Lies and trouble. I no longer
Have any importance. I
Do not miss my horses and
Chariots. Here at home I
Have plenty of pigs and chickens.

LU YOU (1125 – 1209)   51
TRANSLATED BY KENNETH REXROTH

ALBA

When the nightingale to his mate
Sings day-long and night late
My love and I keep state
In bower,
In flower,
'Till the watchman on the tower
Cry:

        "Up! Thou rascal, Rise,
        I see the white
            Light
            And the night
                Flies."

ARNAUT DANIEL (*fl.* LATE 12TH CENTURY)
TRANSLATED BY EZRA POUND

CUCKOO SONG

Sumer is icumen in,
Loude sing cuckou!
Groweth seed and bloweth meed,
And springth the wode now.
Sing cuckou!

Ewe bleteth after lamb,
Loweth after calve cow,
Bulloc sterteth, bucke verteth,
Merye sing cuckou!
Cuckou, cuckou,
Wel singest thou cuckou:
Ne swik thou never now!

---

bloweth meed = meadow blooms
wode = woods
sterteth = leaps
verteth = breaks wind
swik = cease

YESTERDAY I WENT TO HIM FULL OF DISMAY

Yesterday I went to him full of dismay.
He sat silently, not asking what was wrong.

I looked at him, waiting for him to ask,
"How were you yesterday without my luminous face?"

My friend instead was looking at the ground.
Meaning to say, Be like the ground, humble
    and wordless.

I bowed and kissed the ground.
Meaning to say, I am like the ground, drunk
    and amazed.

54   RUMI (1207–73)
    TRANSLATED BY BRAD GOOCH AND
    MARYAM MORTAZ

FOWLS IN THE FRITH

Fowles in the frith,
The fisshes in the flood,
And I mon waxe wood:
Much sorwe I walke with
For beste of boon and blood.

---

fowles = birds
frith = forest
mon waxe wood = must go mad
sorwe = sorrow
beste = best (the poet's beloved)
boon = bone

RONDEAU

Amorous eye,
Bowman of love.

You glance, I die,
Amorous eye;

Your grace: too high
The price thereof,
Amorous eye.

CHRISTINE DE PIZAN (1364 – *c.* 1430)
TRANSLATED BY NORMAN R. SHAPIRO

ROUNDEL: WELCOME SUMMER

Now welcom, summer, with thy sunne softe,
That hast this winters weathers over-shake,
And driven away the longe nyghtes blake.

Saynt Valentyn, that art full high a-lofte,
Thus singen smalle fowles for thy sake.
Now welcom, summer, with thy sunne softe,
That hast this winters weathers over-shake.

Well have they cause for to gladden ofte,
Since each of them recovered hath his make.
Full blissful may they singen when they wake:
Now welcom, summer, with thy sunne softe,
That hast this winters weathers over-shake,
And driven away the longe nyghtes blake.

---

over-shake = overcome
blake = black
make = mate

GEOFFREY CHAUCER (*c.* 1340–1400)   57

THIRTY DAYS HAS NOVEMBER
First-known written version in English

Thirti dayes hath Novembir
April June and Septembir.
Of xxviii is but oon
And alle the remenaunt xxx and i

I AM OF IRELAND

Ich am of Irlonde,
And of the holy londe
   Of Irlonde.
Goode sire, praye ich thee,
For of sainte charitee,
Com and dance with me
   In Irlonde.

---

for of = for the sake of

FALLEN FLOWER

Fallen flower I see
Returning to its branch –
Ah! a butterfly.

SUMMER NIGHT

Summer night –
Sun wide awake:
My eyelids closed.

A SHEPHERD PRAYS TO THE GOD PAN

As a tribute, Pan, to you,
My ewe's carcass here I hang,
She who fell to wolf's sharp fang,
Whom the beast held fast and slew.
Worthy god! If this scapegrace
Moves your heart to tenderness,
Pray give me this year no less
Than a hundred in her place.

PIERRE DE RONSARD (1524–85)   61
TRANSLATED BY NORMAN R. SHAPIRO

WESTERN WIND

Westron wind, when will thou blow?
The small rain down can rain.
Christ, that my love were in my arms,
And I in my bed again.

HEY NONNY NO

Hey nonny no!
Men are fools that wish to die!
Is't not fine to dance and sing
When the bells of death do ring?
Is't not fine to swim in wine,
And turn upon the toe,
And sing hey nonny no,
When the winds do blow,
And the seas do flow?
Hey nonny no!

ANONYMOUS (*c.* 1600)

TWO MADRIGALS

MY LOVE IN HER ATTIRE

My love in her attire doth show her wit,
    It doth so well become her;
For every season she hath dressings fit,
    For winter, spring, and summer.
    No beauty she doth miss
    When all her robes are on;
    But beauty's self she is
    When all her robes are gone.

BROWN IS MY LOVE

    Brown is my love but graceful;
    And each renownèd whiteness,
Matched with thy lovely brown, loseth its brightness.

    Fair is my love, but scornful;
    Yet have I seen despisèd
Dainty white lilies, and sad flowers well prizèd.

SHIPWRECK
From *Epigrams*

After at Sea a tall Ship dyd appere,
Made all of Heben and white Ivorie,
The sailes of Golde, of Silke the tackle were:
Milde was the winde, calme seemed the sea to be:
The Skie eche where did shew full bright and faire.
With riche treasures this gay ship fraighted was.
But sodaine storme did so turmoyle the aire,
And tombled up the sea, that she, alas,
Strake on a rocke that under water lay.
O great misfortune, O great griefe, I say,
Thus in one moment to see lost and drownde
So great riches, as lyke can not be founde.

Heben = Ebony
eche where = everywhere

A DITTY

My true-love hath my heart, and I have his,
By just exchange one for another given:
I hold his dear, and mine he cannot miss,
There never was a better bargain driven:
  My true-love hath my heart, and I have his.

His heart in me keeps him and me in one,
My heart in him his thoughts and senses guides:
He loves my heart, for once it was his own,
I cherish his because in me it bides:
  My true-love hath my heart, and I have his.

ARIEL'S SONG
From *The Tempest*

Where the bee sucks, there suck I.
In a cowslip's bell I lie.
There I couch when owls do cry.
On the bat's back I do fly
After summer merrily.
Merrily, merrily shall I live now
Under the blossom that hangs on the bough.

FULL FATHOM FIVE
From *The Tempest*

Full fathom five thy father lies.
   Of his bones are coral made.
Those are pearls that were his eyes.
   Nothing of him that doth fade
But doth suffer a sea-change
Into something rich and strange.
Sea nymphs hourly ring his knell.
              Ding dong.
Hark! now I hear them: ding dong bell.

WILLIAM SHAKESPEARE (1564–1616)   67

O MISTRESS MINE
From *Twelfth Night*

O mistress mine, where are you roaming?
O, stay and hear! Your truelove's coming,
   That can sing both high and low.
Trip no further, pretty sweeting.
Journeys end in lovers meeting,
   Every wise man's son doth know.

What is love? 'Tis not hereafter.
Present mirth hath present laughter.
   What's to come is still unsure.
In delay there lies no plenty,
Then come kiss me, sweet and twenty.
   Youth's a stuff will not endure.

TELL ME WHERE IS FANCY BRED
From *The Merchant of Venice*

Tell me where is fancy bred,
Or in the heart, or in the head?
How begot, how nourishèd?
   Reply, reply.
It is engendered in the eyes,
With gazing fed, and fancy dies
In the cradle where it lies.
Let us all ring fancy's knell.
I'll begin it. – Ding, dong, bell.
   Ding, dong, bell.

WILLIAM SHAKESPEARE (1564–1616)

GOLDEN SLUMBERS
From *Patient Grissel*

Golden slumbers kiss your eyes,
Smiles awake you when you rise.
Sleep, pretty wantons, do not cry,
And I will sing a lullaby:
Rock them, rock them, lullaby.

Care is heavy, therefore sleep you;
You are care, and care must keep you.
Sleep, pretty wantons, do not cry,
And I will sing a lullaby:
Rock them, rock them, lullaby.

SEVENTEENTH- AND EIGHTEENTH- CENTURY POETS

UPON THE THEME OF LOVE

O Love, how thou art tired out with rhyme!
Thou art a tree whereon all poets climb,
And from thy tender branches everyone
Doth take some fruit, which fancy feeds upon.
But now thy tree is left so bare and poor
That they can hardly gather one plum more.

MARGARET CAVENDISH (1623–73)

A BURNT SHIP

Out of a fired ship, which, by no way
But drowning, could be rescued from the flame,
Some men leap'd forth, and ever as they came
Near the foes' ships, did by their shot decay;
So all were lost, which in the ship were found,
   They in the sea being burnt, they in the burnt ship
      drown'd.

NO MAN IS AN ISLAND
From *Meditation 17*

No man is an island, entire of itself; every man is a
piece of the continent, a part of the main; if a clod be
washed away by the sea, Europe is the less, as well as if
a promontory were, as well as if a manor of thy friend's
or of thine own were; any man's death diminishes me,
because I am involved in mankind, and therefore never
send to know for whom the bell tolls; it tolls for thee.

JOHN DONNE (1572–1631)   73

THE KISS
From *Cynthia's Revels*

O, that joy so soon should waste!
  Or so sweet a bliss
  As a kiss
Might not for ever last!
So sugared, so melting, so soft, so delicious,
  The dew that lies on roses,
  When the morn herself discloses,
Is not so precious.
O, rather than I would it smother,
Were I to taste such another;
  It should be my wishing
  That I might die kissing.

ON MY FIRST SON

Farewell, thou child of my right hand, and joy;
My sin was too much hope of thee, loved boy:
Seven years thou wert lent to me, and I thee pay,
Exacted by thy fate, on the just day.
O could I lose all father now! for why
Will man lament the state he should envy,
To have so soon 'scaped world's and flesh's rage,
And, if no other misery, yet age?
Rest in soft peace, and asked, say, "Here doth lie
Ben Jonson his best piece of poetry."
For whose sake henceforth all his vows be such
As what he loves may never like too much.

BEN JONSON (1572–1637)

CARE-CHARMING SLEEP
From *Valentinian*

Care-charming Sleep, thou easer of all woes,
Brother to Death, sweetly thyself dispose
On this afflicted prince; fall like a cloud
In gentle showers; give nothing that is loud
Or painful to his slumbers; easy, light,
And as a purling stream, thou son of Night,
Pass by his troubled senses; sing his pain,
Like hollow murmuring wind or silver rain;
Into this prince gently, oh, gently slide,
And kiss him into slumbers like a bride.

UPON JULIA'S CLOTHES

Whenas in silks my Julia goes,
Then, then, methinks, how sweetly flows
That liquefaction of her clothes.

Next, when I cast mine eyes and see
That brave vibration each way free;
O how that glittering taketh me!

ON JULIA'S BREATH

Breathe, Julia, breathe, and I'll protest,
  Nay more, I'll deeply swear,
That all the spices of the east
  Are circumfused there.

ROBERT HERRICK (1591 – 1674)   77

UPON A CHILD

Here a pretty baby lies
Sung asleep with lullabies;
Pray be silent, and not stir
Th' easy earth that covers her.

UPON PRUE, HIS MAID

In this little urn is laid
Prudence Baldwin, once my maid,
From whose happy spark here let
Spring the purple violet.

BITTER-SWEET

Ah my dear angry Lord,
Since thou dost love, yet strike;
Cast down, yet help afford;
Sure I will do the like.

I will complain, yet praise;
I will bewail, approve;
And all my sour-sweet days
I will lament, and love.

GEORGE HERBERT (1593–1633)

SONG ON MAY MORNING

Now the bright morning-star, Day's harbinger,
Comes dancing from the East, and leads with her
The flowery May, who from her green lap throws
The yellow cowslip and the pale primrose.
 Hail, bounteous May, that dost inspire
 Mirth, and youth, and warm desire!
 Woods and groves are of thy dressing;
 Hill and dale doth boast thy blessing.
Thus we salute thee with our early song,
And welcome thee, and wish thee long.

TO MY DEAR AND LOVING HUSBAND

If ever two were one, then surely we.
If ever man were loved by wife, then thee;
If ever wife was happy in a man,
Compare with me ye women if you can.
I prize thy love more than whole mines of gold,
Or all the riches that the East doth hold.
My love is such that rivers cannot quench,
Nor ought but love from thee give recompense.
Thy love is such I can no way repay;
The heavens reward thee manifold, I pray.
Then while we live, in love let's so persever,
That when we live no more we may live ever.

ANNE BRADSTREET (1612–72)

TO THE INFANT MARTYRS

Go, smiling souls, your new-built cages break.
In heaven you'll learn to sing, ere here to speak,
Nor let the milky fonts that bathe your thirst
                Be your delay;
The place that calls you hence is, at the worst,
                Milk all the way.

UPON THE INFANT MARTYRS

To see both blended in one flood,
The mothers' milk, the children's blood,
Makes me doubt if heaven will gather
Roses hence, or lilies rather.

TO LUCASTA, GOING TO THE WARS

Tell me not, sweet, I am unkind,
    That from the nunnery
Of thy chaste breast and quiet mind,
    To war and arms I fly.

True, a new mistress now I chase,
    The first foe in the field;
And with a stronger faith embrace
    A sword, a horse, a shield.

Yet this inconstancy is such
    As you too shall adore;
I could not love thee, dear, so much,
    Loved I not honour more.

RICHARD LOVELACE (1618–57)

SONG SUNG BY AERIAL SPIRITS
From *The Indian Queen*

Poor mortals that are clogged with earth below
    Sink under love and care,
    While we that dwell in air
    Such heavy passions never know.
    Why then should mortals be
    Unwilling to be free
    From blood, that sullen cloud
    Which shining souls does shroud?
      Then they'll show bright,
      And like us light,
    When leaving bodies with their care,
    They slide to us and air.

FOUR HAIKU

The old pond:
A frog jumps in, –
The sound of water.

Ah! Summer grasses!
All that remains
Of the warriors' dreams.

Autumn evening;
A crow perched
On a withered bough.

The leeks
Newly washed white –
How cold it is.

MATSUO BASHŌ (1644–94)
TRANSLATED BY R. H. BLYTH

ON MYSELF

Good heaven, I thank thee, since it was designed
I should be framed but of the weaker kind,
That yet my soul is rescued from the love
Of all those trifles, which their passions move.
Pleasures, and praise, and plenty have with me
But their just value. If allowed they be,
Freely and thankfully as much I taste,
As will not reason or religion waste.
If they're denied, I on myself can live,
And slight those aids unequal chance does give.
When in the sun, my wings can be displayed,
And, in retirement, I can bless the shade.

---

line 2: *weaker kind = women*
line 4: *their = women's*

From VERSES MADE FOR FRUIT-WOMEN

APPLES

Come buy my fine wares,
Plums, apples, and pears.
A hundred a penny,
In conscience too many:
Come, will you have any?
My children are seven,
I wish them in Heaven;
My husband a sot,
With his pipe and his pot,
Not a farthing will gain them,
And I must maintain them.

ORANGES

Come buy my fine oranges, sauce for your veal,
And charming, when squeezed in a pot of brown ale;
Well roasted, with sugar and wine in a cup,
They'll make a sweet bishop when gentlefolks sup.

JONATHAN SWIFT (1667 – 1745)   87

UPON A GIRL OF SEVEN YEARS OLD

Wit's queen (if what the poets sing be true)
And beauty's goddess childhood never knew;
Pallas, they say, sprung from the head of Jove
Full grown, and from the sea the Queen of Love;
But had they, Miss, your wit and beauty seen,
Venus and Pallas both had children been.
They, from the sweetness of that radiant look,
A copy of young Venus might have took,
And from those pretty things you speak have told
How Pallas talked when she was seven years old.

FOUR HAIKU

morning glory –
the well-bucket entangled
I ask for water

a hundred gourds
from the heart
of one vine

everything I pick up
is alive –
ebb tide

sleeping alone
awakened
by the frosty night . . .

FUKUDA CHIYO-NI (1703−75)   89
TRANSLATED BY PATRICIA DONEGAN AND
YOSHIE ISHIBASHI

FOUR HAIKU

Lighting one candle
with another candle —
spring evening.

They end their flight
one by one —
crows at dusk.

I go,
you stay;
two autumns.

Blow of an ax,
pine scent,
the winter woods.

90   YOSA BUSON (1716–83)
TRANSLATED BY ROBERT HASS

From TOMMY THUMB'S PRETTY SONG BOOK

SING A SONG OF SIXPENCE

Sing a song of Sixpence,
A bag full of Rye,
Four and twenty
Naughty boys,
Bak'd in a Pye.

GIRLS AND BOYS

Girls and Boys,
Come out to play,
The Moon does shine,
As bright as Day,
Come with a Hoop,
Come with a Call,
Come with a good will,
Or not at all.

ANONYMOUS (*c.* 1744)   91

WAYFARER'S NIGHT SONG

Over the hilltops all
Is still,
Hardly a breath
Seems to ruffle
Any tree crest;
In the wood not one small bird's song.
Only wait, before long
You too will rest.

ALL THINGS THE GODS BESTOW

All things the gods bestow, the infinite ones,
On their darlings completely,
All the joys, the infinite ones,
All the pains, the infinite ones, completely.

THREE EPIGRAMS

UPON THE DEATH OF SIR ALBERT MORTON'S WIFE

He first deceased; she for a little tried
To live without him, liked it not, and died.

SIR HENRY WOTTON (1568–1639)

IMPROMPTU ON CHARLES II

God bless our good and gracious King,
   Whose promise none relies on;
Who never said a foolish thing,
   Nor ever did a wise one.

JOHN WILMOT, EARL OF ROCHESTER (1647–80)

EPIGRAM ENGRAVED ON THE COLLAR OF A DOG
WHICH I GAVE TO HIS ROYAL HIGHNESS

I am his Highness' Dog at Kew;
Pray tell me, Sir, whose Dog are you?

ALEXANDER POPE (1699–1744)

ON BEING BROUGHT FROM
AFRICA TO AMERICA

'Twas mercy brought me from my *Pagan* land,
Taught my benighted soul to understand
That there's a God, that there's a *Saviour* too:
Once I redemption neither sought nor knew.
Some view our sable race with scornful eye,
"Their colour is a diabolic die."
Remember, *Christians*, *Negros*, black as *Cain*,
May be refin'd, and join th' angelic train.

FOUR HAIKU

Don't worry, spiders,
I keep house
　casually.

The snow is melting
and the village is flooded
　with children.

Climb Mount Fuji,
O snail,
　but slowly, slowly.

Mother I never knew
every time I see the ocean,
　every time –

KOBAYASHI ISSA (1763–1827)
TRANSLATED BY ROBERT HASS

THE PLOUGHMAN'S LIFE

As I was a-wand'ring ae morning in spring,
I heard a young ploughman sae sweetly to sing;
And as he was singin', thir words he did say –
"There's nae life like the ploughman's in the month
      o' sweet May.

The lav'rock in the morning she'll rise frae her nest,
And mount i' the air wi' the dew on her breast,
And wi' the merry ploughman she'll whistle and sing,
And at night she'll return to her nest back again."

ANNA, THY CHARMS

Anna, thy charms my bosom fire,
   And waste my soul with care;
But ah! how bootless to admire,
   When fated to despair!

Yet in thy presence, lovely Fair,
   To hope may be forgiven;
For sure 'twere impious to despair
   So much in sight of heaven.

96   ROBERT BURNS (1759–96)

INFANT JOY

I have no name
I am but two days old –
What shall I call thee?
I happy am
Joy is my name –
Sweet joy befall thee!

Pretty joy!
Sweet joy but two days old,
Sweet joy I call thee;
Thou dost smile,
I sing the while:
Sweet joy befall thee!

WILLIAM BLAKE (1757 – 1827)   97

INFANT SORROW

My mother groan'd! my father wept.
Into the dangerous world I leapt:
Helpless, naked, piping loud;
Like a fiend hid in a cloud.

Struggling in my father's hands,
Striving against my swaddling bands;
Bound and weary I thought best
To sulk upon my mother's breast.

ETERNITY

He who binds to himself a joy
Does the winged life destroy;
But he who kisses the joy as it flies
Lives in eternity's sun rise.

THE SICK ROSE

O Rose thou art sick.
The invisible worm
That flies in the night
In the howling storm,

Has found out thy bed
Of crimson joy;
And his dark secret love
Does thy life destroy.

WILLIAM BLAKE (1757 – 1827)

From MOTHER GOOSE'S MELODY

RIDE A COCK HORSE

Ride a cock horse
To *Banbury* cross,
   To see what *Tommy* can buy,
A penny white loaf,
A penny white cake,
   And a two-penny apple-pye.

JACK AND GILL

Jack and *Gill*
Went up the hill,
   To fetch a pail of water.
Jack fell down
And broke his crown,
   And *Gill* came tumbling after.

NINETEENTH-CENTURY POETS

WISHES

Go, little book, and wish to all
Flowers in the garden, meat in the hall,
A bin of wine, a spice of wit,
A house with lawns enclosing it,
A living river by the door,
A nightingale in the sycamore.

ROBERT LOUIS STEVENSON (1850–94)

MY HEART LEAPS UP

My heart leaps up when I behold
  A rainbow in the sky:
So was it when my life began;
So is it now I am a man;
So be it when I shall grow old,
  Or let me die!
The Child is father of the Man;
And I could wish my days to be
Bound each to each by natural piety.

A SLUMBER DID MY SPIRIT SEAL

A slumber did my spirit seal;
  I had no human fears:
She seemed a thing that could not feel
  The touch of earthly years.

No motion has she now, no force;
  She neither hears nor sees;
Rolled round in earth's diurnal course,
  With rocks, and stones, and trees.

WILLIAM WORDSWORTH (1770–1850)   103

From JOURNAL WRITTEN AT GRASMERE

Thursday, April 15, 1802. I never saw daffodils so beautiful. They grew among the mossy stones about and above them; some rested their heads upon these stones, as on a pillow, for weariness; and the rest tossed and reeled and danced and seemed as if they verily laughed with the wind that blew upon them over the lake; they looked so gay, ever glancing, ever changing.

Friday, April 30, 1802. The birds were about us on all sides – skobbies, robins, bullfinches. Crows now and then flew over our heads, as we were warned by the sound of the beating of the air above. We stayed till the light of day was going and the little birds had begun to settle their singing. But there was a thrush not far off that seemed to sing louder and clearer than the thrushes had sung when it was quite day.

ANSWER TO A CHILD'S QUESTION

Do you ask what the birds say? The Sparrow,
    the Dove,
The Linnet and Thrush say, "I love and I love!"
In the winter they're silent – the wind is so strong;
What it says, I don't know, but it sings a loud song.
But green leaves, and blossoms, and sunny warm
    weather,
And singing, and loving – all come back together.
But the Lark is so brimful of gladness and love,
The green fields below him, the blue sky above,
That he sings, and he sings; and for ever sings he –
"I love my Love, and my Love loves me!"

ON DONNE'S POETRY

With Donne, whose muse on dromedary trots,
Wreathe iron pokers into true-love knots;
Rhyme's sturdy cripple, fancy's maze and clue,
Wit's forge and fire-blast, meaning's press and screw.

JENNY KISSED ME

Jenny kissed me when we met,
    Jumping from the chair she sat in;
Time, you thief, who love to get
    Sweets into your list, put that in:
Say I'm weary, say I'm sad,
    Say that health and wealth have missed me,
Say I'm growing old, but add,
    Jenny kissed me.

SO WE'LL GO NO MORE A ROVING

So we'll go no more a roving
  So late into the night,
Though the heart be still as loving,
  And the moon be still as bright.

For the sword outwears its sheath,
  And the soul wears out the breast,
And the heart must pause to breathe,
  And Love itself have rest.

Though the night was made for loving,
  And the day returns too soon,
Yet we'll go no more a roving
  By the light of the moon.

GEORGE GORDON, LORD BYRON (1788 – 1824)   107

MUSIC, WHEN SOFT VOICES DIE

Music, when soft voices die,
Vibrates in the memory –
Odours, when sweet violets sicken,
Live within the sense they quicken.

Rose leaves, when the rose is dead,
Are heaped for the beloved's bed;
And so thy thoughts, when thou art gone,
Love itself shall slumber on.

TO THE MOON

Art thou pale for weariness
Of climbing Heaven, and gazing on the earth,
Wandering companionless
Among the stars that have a different birth, –
And ever changing, like a joyless eye
That finds no object worth its constancy?

THIS LIVING HAND

This living hand, now warm and capable
Of earnest grasping, would, if it were cold
And in the icy silence of the tomb,
So haunt thy days and chill thy dreaming nights
That thou wouldst wish thine own heart dry of blood
So in my veins red life might stream again,
And thou be conscience-calmed – see here it is –
I hold it towards you.

I HAD A DOVE

I had a dove, and the sweet dove died,
    And I have thought it died of grieving;
O what could it grieve for? Its feet were tied
    With a silken thread of my own hand's weaving:
Sweet little red feet! Why would you die?
Why would you leave me, sweet bird, why?
You lived alone in the forest tree,
Why, pretty thing, could you not live with me?
I kissed you oft, and gave you white peas;
Why not live sweetly as in the green trees?

I LOVED YOU

I loved you; and perhaps I love you still,
The flame, perhaps, is not extinguished; yet
It burns so quietly within my soul,
No longer should you feel distressed by it.
Silently and hopelessly I loved you,
At times too jealous and at times too shy.
God grant you find another who will love you
As tenderly and truthfully as I.

ALEXANDER PUSHKIN (1799–1837)
TRANSLATED BY D. M. THOMAS

BEST

What's the best thing in the world?
June-rose, by May-dew impearled;
Sweet south-wind, that means no rain;
Truth, not cruel to a friend;
Pleasure, not in haste to end;
Beauty, not self-decked and curled
Till its pride is over-plain;
Light, that never makes you wink;
Memory, that gives no pain;
Love, when, *so*, you're loved again.
What's the best thing in the world?
– Something out of it, I think.

THE EAGLE

He clasps the crag with crookèd hands;
Close to the sun in lonely lands,
Ringed with the azure world, he stands.

The wrinkled sea beneath him crawls;
He watches from his mountain walls,
And like a thunderbolt he falls.

FLOWER IN THE CRANNIED WALL

Flower in the crannied wall,
I pluck you out of the crannies,
I hold you here, root and all, in my hand,
Little flower – but *if* I could understand
What you are, root and all, all in all,
I should know what God and man is.

ALFRED, LORD TENNYSON (1809–92)   113

MEETING AT NIGHT

The grey sea and the long black land;
And the yellow half-moon large and low;
And the startled little waves that leap
In fiery ringlets from their sleep,
As I gain the cove with pushing prow,
And quench its speed in the slushy sand.

Then a mile of warm sea-scented beach;
Three fields to cross till a farm appears;
A tap at the pane, the quick sharp scratch
And blue spurt of a lighted match,
And a voice less loud, through its joys and fears,
Than the two hearts beating each to each!

PARTING AT MORNING

Round the cape of a sudden came the sea,
And the sun looked over the mountain's rim:
And straight was a path of gold for him,
And the need of a world of men for me.

LOVE AND FRIENDSHIP

Love is like the wild rose-briar,
Friendship like the holly-tree –
The holly is dark when the rose-briar blooms
But which will bloom most constantly?

The wild rose-briar is sweet in spring,
Its summer blossoms scent the air;
Yet wait till winter comes again
And who will call the wild-briar fair?

Then scorn the silly rose-wreath now
And deck thee with the holly's sheen,
That when December blights thy brow
He still may leave thy garland green.

HOW DOTH THE LITTLE CROCODILE

How doth the little crocodile
   Improve his shining tail,
And pour the waters of the Nile
   On every golden scale!

How cheerfully he seems to grin
   How neatly spreads his claws,
And welcomes little fishes in,
   With gently smiling jaws!

THE OWL AND THE PANTHER

I passed by his garden, and marked, with one eye,
How the Owl and the Panther were sharing a pie:
The Panther took pie-crust, and gravy, and meat,
While the Owl had the dish as its share of the treat.
When the pie was all finished, the Owl, as a boon,
Was kindly permitted to pocket the spoon:
While the Panther received knife and fork with a growl.
And concluded the banquet by—

TWO LIMERICKS

THE LADY AND THE TIGER

There was a young lady of Riga,
Who smiled as she rode on a tiger:
    They returned from the ride
    With the lady inside,
And a smile on the face of the tiger.

COSMO MONKHOUSE (1840 – 1901)

AVIARY

There was an Old Man with a beard,
Who said: "It is just as I feared!
    Two Owls and a Hen,
    Four Larks and a Wren,
Have all built their nests in my beard."

EDWARD LEAR (1812 – 88)

MONODY

To have known him, to have loved him
    After loneness long;
And then to be estranged in life,
    And neither in the wrong;
And now for death to set his seal –
    Ease me, a little ease, my song!

By wintry hills his hermit-mound
    The sheeted snow-drifts drape,
And houseless there the snow-bird flits
    Beneath the fir-trees' crape:
Glazed now with ice the cloistral vine
    That hid the shyest grape.

A NOISELESS PATIENT SPIDER

A noiseless patient spider,
I marked where on a little promontory it stood isolated,
Marked how to explore the vacant vast surrounding,
It launched forth filament, filament, filament, out
    of itself,
Ever unreeling them, ever tirelessly speeding them.

And you O my soul where you stand,
Surrounded, detached, in measureless oceans of space,
Ceaselessly musing, venturing, throwing, seeking the
    spheres to connect them,
Till the bridge you will need be formed, till the
    ductile anchor hold,
Till the gossamer thread you fling catch somewhere,
    O my soul.

WALT WHITMAN (1819—92)   119

A GLIMPSE

A glimpse through an interstice caught,
Of a crowd of workmen and drivers in a bar-room
    around the stove late of a winter night, and I
    unremarked seated in a corner,
Of a youth who loves me and whom I love, silently
    approaching and seating himself near, that he
    may hold me by the hand,
A long while amid the noises of coming and going, of
    drinking and oath and smutty jest,
There we two, content, happy in being together,
    speaking little, perhaps not a word.

TO OLD AGE

I see in you the estuary that enlarges and spreads
    itself grandly as it pours in the great Sea.

I'M NOBODY

I'm nobody! Who are you?
Are you – Nobody – too?
Then there's a pair of us!
Don't tell! they'd advertise – you know!

How dreary – to be – Somebody!
How public – like a Frog –
To tell one's name – the livelong June –
To an admiring Bog!

EMILY DICKINSON (1830–86)   121

WILD NIGHTS

Wild nights – Wild nights!
Were I with thee
Wild nights should be
Our luxury!

Futile – the winds –
To a Heart in port –
Done with the Compass –
Done with the Chart!

Rowing in Eden –
Ah – the Sea!
Might I but moor – tonight –
In thee!

AFTER GREAT PAIN

After great pain, a formal feeling comes –
The Nerves sit ceremonious, like Tombs –
The stiff Heart questions "was it He, that bore,"
And "Yesterday, or Centuries before"?

The Feet, mechanical, go round –
A Wooden way
Of Ground, or Air, or Ought –
Regardless grown,
A Quartz contentment, like a stone –

This is the Hour of Lead –
Remembered, if outlived,
As Freezing persons, recollect the Snow –
First – Chill – then Stupor – then the letting go –

EMILY DICKINSON (1830–86)   123

SLEEPING AT LAST

Sleeping at last, the trouble and tumult over,
   Sleeping at last, the struggle and horror past,
Cold and white, out of sight of friend and of lover,
          Sleeping at last.

  No more a tired heart downcast or overcast,
No more pangs that wring or shifting fears that hover,
   Sleeping at last in a dreamless sleep locked fast.

Fast asleep. Singing birds in their leafy cover
   Cannot wake her, nor shake her the gusty blast.
Under the purple thyme and the purple clover
          Sleeping at last.

PIED BEAUTY

Glory be to God for dappled things –
　　For skies of couple-colour as a brinded cow;
　　　For rose-moles all in stipple upon trout that swim;
Fresh-firecoal chestnut-falls; finches' wings;
　　Landscape plotted and pieced – fold, fallow, and plough;
　　　And áll trádes, their gear and tackle and trim.

All things counter, original, spare, strange;
　　Whatever is fickle, freckled (who knows how?)
　　　With swift, slow; sweet, sour; adazzle, dim;
He fathers-forth whose beauty is past change:
　　　　　Praise him.

TANTALIZED

The prison wing that I am quartered in
Faces a railroad station, and the din
Of the machinery, the coupling trains,
Lull my long nights – sleepless for all my pains:
Clattering nests for gods of coal, glass, steel . . .
My mind fancies young birds that chatter, squeal,
Ready to take their flight, untrammeled; fly
Up, up into the still dark, dawn-tinged sky
Above the plains' deep mauve obscurity.
O trains that can go rolling, rolling free!

TRANSLATED BY NORMAN R. SHAPIRO

REQUIEM

Under the wide and starry sky,
Dig the grave and let me lie.
Glad did I live and gladly die,
    And I laid me down with a will.

This be the verse you grave for me:
Here he lies where he longed to be;
Home is the sailor, home from sea,
    And the hunter home from the hill.

MANY RED DEVILS RAN FROM MY HEART

Many red devils ran from my heart
And out upon the page.
They were so tiny
The pen could mash them.
And many struggled in the ink.
It was strange
To write in this red muck
Of things from my heart.

IN THE DESERT

In the desert
I saw a creature, naked, bestial,
Who, squatting upon the ground,
Held his heart in his hands,
And ate of it.
I said: "Is it good, friend?"
"It is bitter – bitter," he answered;
"But I like it
Because it is bitter,
And because it is my heart."

128   STEPHEN CRANE (1871–1900)

MODERN POETS:
EARLY TWENTIETH
CENTURY

POETRY

I, too, dislike it,
    Reading it, however, with a perfect contempt
        for it, one discovers in
    it, after all, a place for the genuine.

MARIANNE MOORE (1887–1972)

AT TEA

The kettle descants in a cosy drone,
And the young wife looks in her husband's face,
And then at her guest's, and shows in her own
Her sense that she fills an envied place;
And the visiting lady is all abloom,
And says there was never so sweet a room.

And the happy young housewife does not know
That the woman beside her was first his choice,
Till the fates ordained it could not be so . . .
Betraying nothing in look or voice
The guest sits smiling and sips her tea,
And he throws her a stray glance yearningly.

LOVELIEST OF TREES

Loveliest of trees, the cherry now
Is hung with bloom along the bough,
And stands about the woodland ride
Wearing white for Eastertide.

Now, of my threescore years and ten,
Twenty will not come again,
And take from seventy springs a score,
It only leaves me fifty more.

And since to look at things in bloom
Fifty springs are little room,
About the woodlands I will go
To see the cherry hung with snow.

HE WOULD NOT STAY FOR ME

He would not stay for me, and who can wonder?
  He would not stay for me to stand and gaze.
I shook his hand, and tore my heart in sunder,
  And went with half my life about my ways.

WHO ARE YOU, READER?
From *The Gardener*

Who are you, reader, reading my poems a hundred years hence?

I cannot send you one single flower from this wealth of the spring, one single streak of gold from yonder clouds.

Open your doors and look abroad.

From your blossoming garden gather fragrant memories of the vanished flowers of a hundred years before.

In the joy of your heart may you feel the living joy that sang one spring morning, sending its glad voice across a hundred years.

LOGIC
From *Stray Birds*

A mind all logic is like a knife all blade.
It makes the hand bleed that uses it.

RABINDRANATH TAGORE (1861–1941)   133

IONIC

That we've broken their statues,
that we've driven them out of their temples,
doesn't mean at all that the gods are dead.
O land of Ionia, they're still in love with you,
their souls still keep your memory.
When an August dawn wakes over you,
your atmosphere is potent with their life,
and sometimes a young ethereal figure
indistinct, in rapid flight,
wings across your hills.

134   CONSTANTINE CAVAFY (1863–1933)
     TRANSLATED BY EDMUND KEELEY
     AND PHILIP SHERRARD

HE WISHES FOR THE
CLOTHS OF HEAVEN

Had I the heavens' embroidered cloths,
Enwrought with golden and silver light,
The blue and the dim and the dark cloths
Of night and light and the half-light,
I would spread the cloths under your feet:
But I, being poor, have only my dreams;
I have spread my dreams under your feet;
Tread softly because you tread on my dreams.

A DRINKING SONG

Wine comes in at the mouth
And love comes in at the eye;
That's all we shall know for truth
Before we grow old and die.
I lift the glass to my mouth,
I look at you, and I sigh.

TO A SQUIRREL AT KYLE-NA-NO

Come play with me;
Why should you run
Through the shaking tree
As though I'd a gun
To strike you dead?
When all I would do
Is to scratch your head
And let you go.

IN THE SUN

In the sun on my bed after swimming –
In the sun and in the vast reflection of the sun on
    the sea,
  Under my window
And in the reflections and the reflections of the
    reflections
Of the sun and the suns on the sea
  In the mirrors,
After the swim, the coffee, the ideas,
  Naked in the sun on my light-flooded bed
    Naked – alone – mad –
      Me!

PAUL VALÉRY (1871–1945)   137
TRANSLATED BY STEPHEN ROMER

SEAL LULLABY

Oh! hush thee, my baby, the night is behind us,
   And black are the waters that sparkled so green.
The moon, o'er the combers, looks downward to
      find us
   At rest in the hollows that rustle between.
Where billow meets billow, there soft be thy pillow;
   Ah, weary wee flipperling, curl at thy ease!
The storm shall not wake thee, nor shark overtake
      thee,
   Asleep in the arms of the slow-swinging seas.

FOUR HAIKU

A hoe standing there;
No-one to be seen, –
The heat!

Peeling a pear,
Sweet drops trickle down
The knife.

Carrying a girl
Across the river;
The hazy moon.

Early dusk:
The mouth of the toad
Exhales the moon.

MASAOKA SHIKI (1867–1902)
TRANSLATED BY R. H. BLYTH

NOTHING GOLD CAN STAY

Nature's first green is gold,
Her hardest hue to hold.
Her early leaf's a flower;
But only so an hour.
Then leaf subsides to leaf.
So Eden sank to grief,
So dawn goes down to day.
Nothing gold can stay.

FIRE AND ICE

Some say the world will end in fire,
Some say in ice.
From what I've tasted of desire
I hold with those who favor fire.
But if it had to perish twice,
I think I know enough of hate
To say that for destruction ice
Is also great
And would suffice.

OPAL

You are ice and fire,
The touch of you burns my hands like snow.
You are cold and flame.
You are the crimson of amaryllis,
The silver of moon-touched magnolias.
When I am with you,
My heart is a frozen pond
Gleaming with agitated torches.

A DECADE

When you came, you were like red wine and honey,
And the taste of you burnt my mouth with its
        sweetness.
Now you are like morning bread,
Smooth and pleasant.
I hardly taste you at all for I know your savour,
But I am completely nourished.

AMY LOWELL (1874–1925)   141

THE PANTHER
In the Jardin des Plantes, Paris

His vision, from the constantly passing bars,
has grown so weary that it cannot hold
anything else. It seems to him there are
a thousand bars; and behind the bars, no world.

As he paces in cramped circles, over and over,
the movement of his powerful soft strides
is like a ritual dance around a center
in which a mighty will stands paralyzed.

Only at times, the curtain of the pupils
lifts, quietly –. An image enters in,
rushes down through the tensed, arrested muscles,
plunges into the heart and is gone.

142   RAINER MARIA RILKE (1875 – 1926)
TRANSLATED BY STEPHEN MITCHELL

TWO CINQUAINS

NOVEMBER NIGHT

Listen.
With faint dry sound,
Like steps of passing ghosts,
The leaves, frost-crisp'd, break from the trees
And fall.

TRIAD

These be
Three silent things:
The falling snow . . . the hour
Before the dawn . . . the mouth of one
Just dead.

ADELAIDE CRAPSEY (1878–1914)   143

FOG

The fog comes
on little cat feet.

It sits looking
over harbor and city
on silent haunches
and then moves on.

CHOOSE

The single clenched fist lifted and ready,
Or the open asking hand held out and waiting.
                    Choose:
For we meet by one or the other.

GRASS

Pile the bodies high at Austerlitz and Waterloo.
Shovel them under and let me work –
                    I am the grass; I cover all.

And pile them high at Gettysburg
And pile them high at Ypres and Verdun.
Shovel them under and let me work.
Two years, ten years, and passengers ask the
    conductor:
                    What place is this?
                    Where are we now?

                    I am the grass.
                    Let me work.

LIFE IS MOTION

In Oklahoma,
Bonnie and Josie,
Dressed in calico,
Danced around a stump.
They cried,
"Ohoyaho,
Ohoo" . . .
Celebrating the marriage
Of flesh and air.

ANECDOTE OF THE JAR

I placed a jar in Tennessee,
And round it was, upon a hill.
It made the slovenly wilderness
Surround that hill.

The wilderness rose up to it,
And sprawled around, no longer wild.
The jar was round upon the ground
And tall and of a port in air.

It took dominion everywhere.
The jar was gray and bare.
It did not give of bird or bush,
Like nothing else in Tennessee.

OF MERE BEING

The palm at the end of the mind,
Beyond the last thought, rises
In the bronze decor,

A gold-feathered bird
Sings in the palm, without human meaning,
Without human feeling, a foreign song.

You know then that it is not the reason
That makes us happy or unhappy.
The bird sings. Its feathers shine.

The palm stands on the edge of space.
The wind moves slowly in the branches.
The bird's fire-fangled feathers dangle down.

HUMORESQUE

To some the fat gods
Give money,
To some love;

But the gods have given me
Money a n d love:

Not t o o m u c h money,
Nor q u i t e e n o u g h love!

To some the fat gods
Give money,
To some love.

MIRROR

In

ARE · THIS

ONS · MIR

I · ROR

CT · I

LE · AM

REF · EN

AS · Guillaume · CLOSED

NOT · Apollinaire · AL

AND · IVE

GELS · AND

AN · REAL

INE · AS

MAG · YOU

I

TRANSLATED BY ANNE HYDE GREET

A FLOWER GIVEN
TO MY DAUGHTER

Frail the white rose and frail are
Her hands that gave
Whose soul is sere and paler
Than time's wan wave.

Rosefrail and fair – yet frailest
A wonder wild
In gentle eyes thou veilest,
My blueveined child.

JAMES JOYCE (1882 – 1941)   151

From ULYSSES: FOUND POEMS

NIGHT SKY

The heaventree of stars
  hung with humid
nightblue fruit.

YES

I asked him with my eyes to ask again yes and then he
asked me would I yes to say yes my mountain flower
and first I put my arms around him yes and drew him
down to me so he could feel my breasts all perfume
yes and his heart was going like mad and yes I said
yes I will Yes.

JAMES JOYCE (1882–1941)

THE FOX

A fox looked at his shadow at sunrise and said, "I will have a camel for lunch today." And all morning he went about looking for camels. But at noon he saw his shadow again – and he said, "A mouse will do."

THE RED WHEELBARROW

so much depends
upon

a red wheel
barrow

glazed with rain
water

beside the white
chickens

THIS IS JUST TO SAY

I have eaten
the plums
that were in
the icebox

and which
you were probably
saving
for breakfast

Forgive me
they were delicious
so sweet
and so cold

L(A

1(a

le
af
fa

ll

s)
one
l

iness

GREEN

The dawn was apple-green,
   The sky was green wine held up in the sun,
The moon was a golden petal between.

She opened her eyes, and green
   They shone, clear like flowers undone
For the first time, now for the first time seen.

THE GAZELLE CALF

The gazelle calf, O my children,
goes behind its mother across the desert,
goes behind its mother on blithe bare foot
requiring no shoes, O my children!

IN A STATION OF THE METRO

The apparition of these faces in the crowd;
Petals on a wet, black bough.

ALBA

As cool as the pale wet leaves
                    of the lily-of-the-valley
She lay beside me in the dawn.

THE BATH TUB

As a bathtub lined with white porcelain,
When the hot water gives out or goes tepid,
So is the slow cooling of our chivalrous passion,
O my much praised but-not-altogether-satisfactory
    lady.

HEAT

O wind, rend open the heat,
cut apart the heat,
rend it to tatters.

Fruit cannot drop
through this thick air —
fruit cannot fall into heat
that presses up and blunts
the points of pears
and rounds the grapes.

Cut the heat —
plough through it,
turning it on either side
of your path.

TO A SNAIL

If "compression is the first grace of style,"
you have it. Contractility is a virtue
as modesty is a virtue.
It is not the acquisition of any one thing
that is able to adorn,
or the incidental quality that occurs
as a concomitant of something well said,
that we value in style,
but the principle that is hid:
in the absence of feet, "a method of conclusions";
"a knowledge of principles,"
in the curious phenomenon of your occipital horn.

O TO BE A DRAGON

If I, like Solomon, . . .
    could have my wish –

my wish . . . O to be a dragon,
a symbol of the power of Heaven – of silkworm
size or immense; at times invisible.
    Felicitous phenomenon!

MARIANNE MOORE (1887–1972)   161

From PRELUDES

I

The winter evening settles down
With smell of steaks in passageways.
Six o'clock.
The burnt-out ends of smoky days.
And now a gusty shower wraps
The grimy scraps
Of withered leaves about your feet
And newspapers from vacant lots;
The showers beat
On broken blinds and chimney-pots,
And at the corner of the street
A lonely cab-horse steams and stamps.
And then the lighting of the lamps.

MORNING
Santa Maria La Longa, January 26, 1917

Immensity
illumines me

SOLDIERS
Forest of Courton, July, 1918

We are as –
in autumn
on the trees –
leaves

GIUSEPPE UNGARETTI (1888–1970)   163
TRANSLATED BY ALLEN MANDELBAUM

HOPS

Beneath the willow, wound round with ivy,
We take cover from the worst
Of the storm, with a greatcoat round
Our shoulders and my hands around your waist.

I've got it wrong. That isn't ivy
Entwined in the bushes round
The wood, but hops. You intoxicate me!
Let's spread the greatcoat on the ground.

THE PILLOW HOT

The pillow hot
On both sides,
The second candle
Dying, the ravens
Crying. Haven't
Slept all night, too late
To dream of sleep . . .
How unbearably white
The blind on the white window.
Good morning, morning!

ANNA AKHMATOVA (1889–1966)
TRANSLATED BY D. M. THOMAS

THE TROPICS IN NEW YORK

Bananas ripe and green, and ginger-root,
   Cocoa in pods and alligator pears,
And tangerines and mangoes and grape fruit,
   Fit for the highest prize at parish fairs,

Set in the window, bringing memories
   Of fruit-trees laden by low-singing rills,
And dewy dawns, and mystical blue skies
   In benediction over nun-like hills.

My eyes grew dim, and I could no more gaze;
   A wave of longing through my body swept,
And, hungry for the old, familiar ways,
   I turned aside and bowed my head and wept.

FIRST FIG

My candle burns at both ends;
  It will not last the night;
But ah, my foes, and oh, my friends —
  It gives a lovely light!

SECOND FIG

Safe upon the solid rock the ugly houses stand:
Come and see my shining palace built upon the sand!

RÉSUMÉ

Razors pain you;
Rivers are damp;
Acids stain you;
And drugs cause cramp.
Guns aren't lawful;
Nooses give;
Gas smells awful;
You might as well live.

REAPERS

Black reapers with the sound of steel on stones
Are sharpening scythes. I see them place the hones
In their hip-pockets as a thing that's done,
And start their silent swinging, one by one.
Black horses drive a mower through the weeds,
And there, a field rat, startled, squealing bleeds,
His belly close to ground. I see the blade,
Blood-stained, continue cutting weeds and shade.

From NIGHT
(*Suite for Piano and Poet's Voice*)

SWATH

O St. James Road.
O Milky Way.
(O night of love for me
when the yellow bird was painted
painted
painted
up in the lemontree.)

URSA MAJOR

Bear mother
gives suck to the stars
astride her belly:
Grunt
grunt.
Run off, star babies,
tender little stars.

FAREWELL

If I die,
leave the balcony open.

The boy eats oranges.
(I see him from my balcony).

The harvester reaps the wheat.
(I sense it from my balcony).

If I die,
leave the balcony open!

FEDERICO GARCÍA LORCA (1898–1936)   171
TRANSLATED BY TOMÁS Q. MORÍN

INCIDENT
(*For Eric Walrond*)

Once riding in old Baltimore,
   Heart-filled, head-filled with glee,
I saw a Baltimorean
   Keep looking straight at me.

Now I was eight and very small,
   And he was no whit bigger,
And so I smiled, but he poked out
   His tongue, and called me, "Nigger."

I saw the whole of Baltimore
   From May until December;
Of all the things that happened there
   That's all that I remember.

MODERN POETS: MID-TWENTIETH CENTURY

IN TELEGRAM-STYLE

Longwinded philosophers rarely tire.
Three stanzas and a poet may expire!

MY BEST WORK

My best work as a poet . . .?
I never wrote it.
It rose from deepest depths —
Which I suppressed.

MASCHA KALÉKO (1907–75)
TRANSLATED BY MARY HENNESSY

THE MOON
for María Kodama

There is such loneliness in that gold.
The moon of the nights is not the moon
Whom the first Adam saw. The long centuries
Of human vigil have filled her
With ancient lament. Look at her. She is your mirror.

JORGE LUIS BORGES (1899–1986)   175
TRANSLATED BY WILLIS BARNSTONE

HARLEM

What happens to a dream deferred?

> Does it dry up
> like a raisin in the sun?
> Or fester like a sore –
> And then run?
> Does it stink like rotten meat?
> Or crust and sugar over –
> like a syrupy sweet?
>
> Maybe it just sags
> like a heavy load.
>
> *Or does it explode?*

POEM (*To F.S.*)

I loved my friend.
He went away from me.
There's nothing more to say.
The poem ends,
Soft as it began, –
I loved my friend.

SUICIDE NOTE

The calm,
Cool face of the river
Asked me for a kiss.

REFLECTION ON ICE-BREAKING

Candy
Is dandy
But liquor
Is quicker.

THE LAMA

The one-l lama,
He's a priest.
The two-l llama,
He's a beast.
And I will bet
A silk pajama
There isn't any
Three-l lllama.

NOT WAVING BUT DROWNING

Nobody heard him, the dead man,
But still he lay moaning:
I was much further out than you thought
And not waving but drowning.

Poor chap, he always loved larking
And now he's dead
It must have been too cold for him his heart gave way,
They said.

Oh, no no no, it was too cold always
(Still the dead one lay moaning)
I was much too far out all my life
And not waving but drowning.

STEVIE SMITH (1902–71)   179

POET'S WORK

Grandfather
  advised me:
    Learn a trade

I learned
  to sit at desk
    and condense

No layoff
  from this
    condensery

A MONSTER OWL

A monster owl
out on the fence
flew away. What
is it the sign
of? The sign of
an owl.

MARCH

Bird feeder's
    snow-cap
        sliding
            off

OCTOPI

Oh octopus, oh fierce monk,
the trembling of your garb
flows across the salt of the rock,
satanic and slippery.
Oh visceral testimony,
branch of frozen rays,
head of a monarchy
all arms and foreboding:
portrait of shivering,
plural cloud of black rain.

TRANSLATED BY MARTÍN ESPADA

FROM THE PERSIAN (1)

Naked out of the dark we came.
Naked into the dark we go.
Come to my arms, naked in the dark.

FROM THE PERSIAN (2)

You are like the moon except
For your dark hair. You are like
Venus, except for your lips,
Crimson and perfumed, and like
The sun, except that you are
Most splendid naked, at night.

THAT NIGHT WHEN JOY BEGAN

That night when joy began
Our narrowest veins to flush,
We waited for the flash
Of morning's levelled gun.

But morning let us pass,
And day by day relief
Outgrows his nervous laugh,
Grown credulous of peace,

As mile by mile is seen
No trespasser's reproach,
And love's best glasses reach
No fields but are his own.

EPITAPH ON A TYRANT

Perfection, of a kind, was what he was after,
And the poetry he invented was easy to understand;
He knew human folly like the back of his hand,
And was greatly interested in armies and fleets;
When he laughed, respectable senators burst with
    laughter,
And when he cried the little children died in the
    streets.

AUGUST 1968

The Ogre does what ogres can,
Deeds quite impossible for Man,
But one prize is beyond his reach,
The Ogre cannot master Speech.
About a subjugated plain,
Among its desperate and slain,
The Ogre stalks with hands on hips,
While drivel gushes from his lips.

W. H. AUDEN (1907–73)   185

From SHORTS

GIVE ME A DOCTOR

Give me a doctor, partridge-plump,
Short in the leg and broad in the rump,
An endomorph with gentle hands,
Who'll never make absurd demands
That I abandon all my vices,
Nor pull a long face in a crisis,
But with a twinkle in his eye
Will tell me that I have to die.

SCANDAL

A Young Person came out of the mists,
Who had the most beautiful wrists:
   A scandal occurred
   Which has long been interred,
But the legend about them persists.

TWO LIMERICKS

THE PELICAN

A wonderful bird is the pelican,
His bill can hold more than his belican.
  He can hold in his beak
  Food enough for a week;
Though I'm damned if I see how the helican!

DIXON MERRITT (1879–1972)

THEORY OF RELATIVITY

There was a young lady named Bright
Whose speed was far faster than light;
  She set out one day
  In a relative way
And returned on the previous night.

A. H. R. BULLER (1874–1944)

FOUR HAIKU

For you, O gulls,
I order slaty waters
    And this leaden sky!

Make up your mind, Snail!
You are half inside your house,
    And halfway out!

In the falling snow
A laughing boy holds out his palms
    Until they are white.

Fire-fly, why play here?
The boys and girls are in the backyard,
    Waiting for you.

CHILD ON TOP OF A GREENHOUSE

The wind billowing out the seat of my britches,
My feet crackling splinters of glass and dried putty,
The half-grown chrysanthemums staring up like
    accusers,
Up through the streaked glass, flashing with sunlight,
A few white clouds all rushing eastward,
A line of elms plunging and tossing like horses,
And everyone, everyone pointing up and shouting!

THEODORE ROETHKE (1908–63)

CASABIANCA

Love's the boy stood on the burning deck
trying to recite "The boy stood on
the burning deck." Love's the son
    stood stammering elocution
    while the poor ship in flames went down.

Love's the obstinate boy, the ship,
even the swimming sailors, who
would like a schoolroom platform, too,
    or an excuse to stay
    on deck. And love's the burning boy.

THE DEATH OF THE BALL TURRET GUNNER

From my mother's sleep I fell into the State,
And I hunched in its belly till my wet fur froze.
Six miles from earth, loosed from its dream of life,
I woke to black flak and the nightmare fighters.
When I died they washed me out of the turret with
    a hose.

THE STREET

A long and silent street.
I walk in blackness and I stumble and fall
and rise, and I walk blind, my feet
stepping on silent stones and dry leaves.
Someone behind me also stepping on stones, leaves:
if I slow down, he slows;
if I run, he runs. I turn: nobody.
Everything dark and doorless.
Turning and turning among these corners
which lead forever to the street
where nobody waits for, nobody follows me,
where I pursue a man who stumbles
and rises and says when he sees me: nobody.

TRANSLATED BY MURIEL RUKEYSER

WE REAL COOL

The pool players.
Seven at the Golden Shovel.

We real cool. We
Left school. We

Lurk late. We
Strike straight. We

Sing sin. We
Thin gin. We

Jazz June. We
Die soon.

FOUR HAIKU

Useless! useless!
  – heavy rain driving
Into the sea

In my medicine cabinet
  the winter fly
Has died of old age

The summer chair
  rocking by itself
In the blizzard

Missing a kick
  at the icebox door
It closed anyway

DAYS

What are days for?
Days are where we live.
They come, they wake us
Time and time over.
They are to be happy in:
Where can we live but days?

Ah, solving that question
Brings the priest and the doctor
In their long coats
Running over the fields.

THIS BE THE VERSE

They fuck you up, your mum and dad.
    They may not mean to, but they do.
They fill you with the faults they had
    And add some extra, just for you.

But they were fucked up in their turn
    By fools in old-style hats and coats,
Who half the time were soppy-stern
    And half at one another's throats.

Man hands on misery to man.
    It deepens like a coastal shelf.
Get out as early as you can,
    And don't have any kids yourself.

CUT GRASS

Cut grass lies frail:
Brief is the breath
Mown stalks exhale.
Long, long the death

It dies in the white hours
Of young-leafed June
With chestnut flowers,
With hedges snowlike strewn,

White lilac bowed,
Lost lanes of Queen Anne's lace,
And that high-builded cloud
Moving at summer's pace.

PHILIP LARKIN (1922—85)   197

BLESSED BE THE MUSES

    for their descent,
dancing round my desk,
crowning my balding head
    with Laurel.

            1955

FOURTH FLOOR, DAWN,
UP ALL NIGHT WRITING LETTERS

Pigeons shake their wings on the copper church roof
out my window across the street, a bird perched on
    the cross
surveys the city's blue-gray clouds. Larry Rivers
'll come at 10 A.M. and take my picture. I'm taking
your picture, pigeons. I'm writing you down, Dawn.
I'm immortalizing your exhaust, Avenue A bus.
O Thought, now you'll have to think the same thing
    forever!

        New York, June 7, 1980, 6:48 A.M.

ANIMALS

Have you forgotten what we were like then
when we were still first rate
and the day came fat with an apple in its mouth

it's no use worrying about Time
but we did have a few tricks up our sleeves
and turned some sharp corners

the whole pasture looked like our meal
we didn't need speedometers
we could manage cocktails out of ice and water

I wouldn't want to be faster
or greener than now if you were with me O you
were the best of all my days

FRANK O'HARA (1926–66)

THE FIELDS FOR MILES

The fields were misted with the cold for miles;
a devilish frost outlined hedge and roof
and dwindling stack, sharp as white acid,
not the showier and somehow reassuring ruff
of snow. I travelled that morning through
the southern shires by train, along embankments
and on levels where I saw the land laid out,
and what I most remember about
that winter is not that it was hard
and cruel after war but that, one morning,
from a shabby train, and cold, I saw
along the line and in unseen, remembered counties,
the trees all over England blossoming with frost.

AUTUMN BEGINS IN MARTINS FERRY, OHIO

In the Shreve High football stadium,
I think of Polacks nursing long beers in Tiltonsville,
And gray faces of Negroes in the blast furnace at
    Benwood,
And the ruptured night watchman of Wheeling Steel,
Dreaming of heroes.

All the proud fathers are ashamed to go home.
Their women cluck like starved pullets,
Dying for love.

Therefore,
Their sons grow suicidally beautiful
At the beginning of October,
And gallop terribly against each other's bodies.

JAMES WRIGHT (1927–80)   201

METAPHORS

I'm a riddle in nine syllables,
An elephant, a ponderous house,
A melon strolling on two tendrils.
O red fruit, ivory, fine timbers!
This loaf's big with its yeasty rising.
Money's new-minted in this fat purse.
I'm a means, a stage, a cow in calf.
I've eaten a bag of green apples,
Boarded the train there's no getting off.

CONTEMPORARY POETS

THE OLD POETS OF CHINA

Wherever I am, the world comes after me.
It offers me its busyness. It does not believe
that I do not want it. Now I understand
why the old poets of China went so far and high
into the mountains, then crept into the pale mist.

MARY OLIVER (1935–2019)

SMALL POEM ABOUT THE
HOUNDS AND THE HARES

After the kill, there is the feast.
And toward the end, when the dancing subsides
and the young have sneaked off somewhere,
the hounds, drunk on the blood of the hares,
begin to talk of how soft
were their pelts, how graceful their leaps,
how lovely their scared, gentle eyes.

LISEL MUELLER (1924–2020)

CLARIFICATIONS

The crows, mingled
powder white,

arrive floundering
through the

heavy snowfall:
they land ruffling

stark black
on the spruce boughs and

chisel the neighborhood
sharp with their cries.

SALUTE

May happiness
pursue you,

catch you
often, and,

should it
lose you,

be waiting
ahead, making

a clearing
for you.

A. R. AMMONS (1926–2001)

I KNOW A MAN

As I sd to my
friend, because I am
always talking, – John, I

sd, which was not his
name, the darkness sur-
rounds us, what

can we do against
it, or else, shall we &
why not, buy a goddamn big car,

drive, he sd, for
christ's sake, look
out where yr going.

FROST

The sky is blank with a single vapour trail
    Warmed by a sunset we cannot see:
The coming freeze is hurrying it away,
    But listen: owls are shaping out the spaces
With their map of sounds. Sparks of stars
    Pierce through where darkness deepens,
Sharp with an undiluted light. Tomorrow we shall
      wake
    At the crackle of first footsteps grinding white.

IN DECEMBER

Cattle are crowding the salt-lick.
The gruel of mud icily thickens.
On the farm-boy's Honda a sweat of fog drops.
They are logging the woodland, the sole standing
      crop.

MACRODOT
A pattern-poem

<pre>
            This is
         a macrodot-shaped
        poem by which we mean
       not merely a disc or an
      emblematic circle which a
      text so figured might claim
      meant sun moon world eternity
      or perfection No Just a blown
      up dot in lines of 7 up to 29
       letters Past the middle the
        lines of type get shorter
         and move faster but all
          adding up to too much
            fuss about making
              a point
</pre>

IN THE EVENING

Three hours chain-smoking words
and you move on. We stand in the porch,
two archaic figures: a woman and a man.

The old masters, the old sources,
haven't a clue what we're about,
shivering here in the half-dark 'sixties.

Our minds hover in a famous impasse
and cling together. Your hand
grips mine like a railing on an icy night.

The wall of the house is bleeding. Firethorn!
The moon, cracked every which-way,
pushes steadily on.

ADRIENNE RICH (1929–2012)   211

SNAILS

Out of earliest ooze, old
Even by sea-stone time,
Slimed as eels, wrinkled as whales,
And cold
As dogs' noses,
And slow, sap-slow,
Under their coiled cauls of shells
Snails
Climb
The roses

THE TOUCAN

Tell me who can
Catch a toucan?
Lou can.

Just how few can
Ride the toucan?
Two can.

What kind of goo can
Stick you to the toucan?
Glue can.

Who can write some
More about the toucan?
You can!

SHEL SILVERSTEIN (1930–99)

THE FIST

The fist clenched round my heart
loosens a little, and I gasp
brightness; but it tightens
again. When have I ever not loved
the pain of love? But this has moved

past love to mania. This has the strong
clench of the madman, this is
gripping the ledge of unreason, before
plunging howling into the abyss.

Hold hard then, heart. This way at least you live.

YOUTH'S PROGRESS

Dick Schneider of Wisconsin . . . was elected
"Greek God" for an interfraternity ball. — *Life*

When I was born, my mother taped my ears
So they lay flat. When I had aged ten years,
My teeth were firmly braced and much improved.
Two years went by; my tonsils were removed.

At fourteen, I began to comb my hair
A fancy way. Though nothing much was there,
I shaved my upper lip — next year, my chin.
At seventeen, the freckles left my skin.

Just turned nineteen, a nicely molded lad,
I said goodbye to Sis and Mother; Dad
Drove me to Wisconsin and set me loose.
At twenty-one, I was elected Zeus.

THE SNOW MARE

In my dream, a blue mare loping,
Pewter on a porcelain field, away.
There are bursts of soft commotion
Where her hooves drive in the drifts,
And as dusk ebbs on the plane of night,
She shears the web of winter,
And on the far, blind side
She is no more. I behold nothing,
Wherein the mare dissolves in memory,
Beyond the burden of being.

ALIENATION

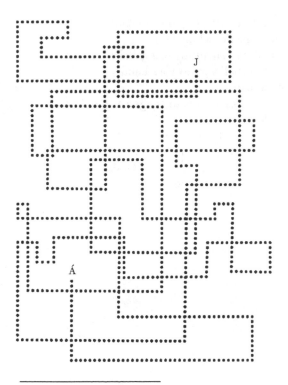

Translation:
JÁ = I

HOMAGE TO MY HAIR

when i feel her jump up and dance
i hear the music! my God
i'm talking about my nappy hair!
she is a challenge to your hand
black man,
she is as tasty on your tongue as good greens
black man,
she can touch your mind
with her electric fingers and
the grayer she do get, good God,
the blacker she do be!

ORIOLE

Emerging after three months to the edge
of the hole of pain I arrange
ten orange halves on a stiff wire
off the patio between a small tree
and the feeder. Early next morning
five orioles of three species appear:
Scott's, hooded, Bullock's. Thinking
of those long nights: this is what agony wanted,
these wildly colored birds to inhabit
my mind far from pain.
Now they live inside me.

AMERICAN HISTORY

Those four black girls blown up
in that Alabama church
remind me of five hundred
middle passage blacks,
in a net, under water
in Charleston harbor
so redcoats wouldn't find them.
Can't find what you can't see
can you?

ON THIS VERY STREET IN BELGRADE

Your mother carried you
Out of the smoking ruins of a building
And set you down on this sidewalk
Like a doll bundled in burnt rags,
Where you now stood years later
Talking to a homeless dog,
Half-hidden behind a parked car,
His eyes brimming with hope
As he inched forward, ready for the worst.

WATERMELONS

Green Buddhas
On the fruit stand.
We eat the smile
And spit out the teeth.

CHARLES SIMIC (1938–)   221

YOU FIT INTO ME

you fit into me
like a hook into an eye

a fish hook
an open eye

LAST YEAR I ABSTAINED

Last year I abstained
this year I devour

without guilt
which is also an art

MOTHER OF THE GROOM

What she remembers
Is his glistening back
In the bath, his small boots
In the ring of boots at her feet.

Hands in her voided lap,
She hears a daughter welcomed.
It's as if he kicked when lifted
And slipped her soapy hold.

Once soap would ease off
The wedding ring
That's bedded forever now
In her clapping hand.

FLOATER

It is always there, the blurry dot,
the mark, so easy to dismiss,
between you and the life you're focused on,
though more distinct with white behind it:
a blowing curtain, a wedding gown,
while pinning bed sheets on a line,
a blank wall in a waiting room, and,
late in life, while leaning on a shovel,
resting, following a heavy snow.

THE MAN FROM WASHINGTON

The end came easy for most of us.
Packed away in our crude beginnings
in some far corner of a flat world,
we didn't expect much more than firewood and
        buffalo robes
to keep us warm. The man came down,
a slouching dwarf with rainwater eyes,
and spoke to us. He promised
that life would go on as usual,
that treaties would be signed, and everyone –
man, woman and child – would be inoculated
against a world in which we had no part,
a world of money, promise and disease.

JAMES WELCH (1940–2003)

BIOGRAPHY

The dog scatters her body in sleep,
paws, finding no ground, whip at air,
the unseen eyeballs reel deep, within.
And waking – crouches,
tacked to humility all day,
children ride her, stretch,
display the black purple lips,
pull hind legs to dance;
unaware that she
tore bulls apart, loosed
heads of partridges,
dreamt blood.

THE ORANGE

At lunchtime I bought a huge orange –
The size of it made us all laugh.
I peeled it and shared it with Robert and Dave –
They got quarters and I had a half.

And that orange, it made me so happy,
As ordinary things often do
Just lately. The shopping. A walk in the park.
This is peace and contentment. It's new.

The rest of the day was quite easy.
I did all the jobs on my list
And enjoyed them and had some time over.
I love you. I'm glad I exist.

WENDY COPE (1945–)

VALENTINE

My heart has made its mind up
And I'm afraid it's you.
Whatever you've got lined up,
My heart has made its mind up
And if you can't be signed up
This year, next year will do.
My heart has made its mind up
And I'm afraid it's you.

ANOTHER UNFORTUNATE CHOICE

I think I am in love with A. E. Housman,
Which puts me in a worse-than-usual fix.
No woman ever stood a chance with Housman
And he's been dead since 1936.

GEOMETRY

I prove a theorem and the house expands:
the windows jerk free to hover near the ceiling,
the ceiling floats away with a sigh.

As the walls clear themselves of everything
but transparency, the scent of carnations
leaves with them. I am out in the open

and above the windows have hinged into butterflies,
sunlight glinting where they've intersected.
They are going to some point true and unproven.

RITA DOVE (1952–)

IMMIGRANT CENTURIES

These are immigrant times
And the lines are long,

The signs for jobs few,
The songs sadder, the air meaner.

Everyone is hungry.
Everyone is willing.

Jobs are not jobs but lives lived
Hard at the work of being human.

These are immigrant times,
And the lines are long again.

From THE ELEMENTS OF SAN JOAQUIN
For César Chávez

FIELD

The wind sprays pale dirt into my mouth
The small, almost invisible scars
On my hands.

The pores in my throat and elbows
Have taken in a seed of dirt of their own.

After a day in the grape fields near Rolinda
A fine silt, washed by sweat,
Has settled into the lines
On my wrists and palms.

Already I am becoming the valley,
A soil that sprouts nothing.
For any of us.

RURAL SCENE

The luminous Norfolk skies,
the tractors, the gunshots,
the still ponds, the darting rabbits,
cow parsley by the field gates –

all are re-imagining themselves
because Tariq walks in his village,
part of the scene, yet conspicuous,
as if he is walking a tiger.

THE BODY AS BRAILLE

He tells me, "Your back
is so beautiful." He traces
my spine with his hand.

I'm burning like the white ring
around the moon. "A witch's moon,"
dijo mi abuela. The schools call it

"a reflection of ice crystals."
It's a storm brewing in the cauldron
of the sky. I'm in love

but won't tell him
if it's omens
or ice.

From THE RODRIGO POEMS

THE WORLD WITHOUT RODRIGO

moves
at a slender pace
does not mind to hesitate
undoes one button
exhales with grace
walks does not run
hums

RODRIGO RETURNS TO THE LAND AND LINEN CELEBRATES

puffed with air
the muslin and satin
the fitted and flat
the dizzy percale
and spun cotton
billowing and snapping
sun-plumped and flapping
everywhere! everywhere!

234 SANDRA CISNEROS (1954–)

STRANGE PLACE

I watch you undress by household candlelight.
We are having an early night. On the wireless
news from other countries half distracts me.

Each small movement makes a longer shadow
on the wall. I lie here quietly as garments fall.
A faint voice talks of weather somewhere else.

But we are here and now, listening to nothing blindly,
where there is no news or weather. Love, later,
I will feel homesick for this strange place.

CAROL ANN DUFFY (1955–)

APRIL MOON

The moon tonight is closer to us
than it will be
for the rest of the year,
grace willing, the year
we will remember as the Great Pandemic.
Pulling us closer into its orbit,
shining the light of its fullness into the room,
we turn to hold in our hands
each other's face as if
for the first time,
and the last –
Pink Moon, Egg Moon, Moon of New Grass.

BEGGING THE QUESTION

The yellow tom is running with his head thrown
back, among the trees the cows have rubbed
their necks on. The rabbit in his jaws is gray
and wobbling. The cat's leg must be only barely
healed, bitten out above the paw last week. The red
roses that I bought you, love, are dropping,
barely open. I'm watching from the chair.
The cat is no more angry at the rabbit than
the cattle at the grass. Come and eat.

EATING TOGETHER

In the steamer is the trout
seasoned with slivers of ginger,
two sprigs of green onion, and sesame oil.
We shall eat it with rice for lunch,
brothers, sister, my mother who will
taste the sweetest meat of the head,
holding it between her fingers
deftly, the way my father did
weeks ago. Then he lay down
to sleep like a snow-covered road
winding through pines older than him,
without any travelers, and lonely for no one.

OF APRIL
after Audubon's "Marsh Wren"

like light
down a canyon,

like treefall,

thought

opens itself

on spring –

marsh wrens

chittering
from the rushes

HOMEWORK

It's evening again, late.
I go out into the lane
and doodle a beard and mustache
on the face of the moon
with a red pen.

Over the next hill
an old teacher of mine
takes off her glasses
and wipes the lenses with a soft cloth.
She can't believe
what she's just seen.

"SINNERS IN THE HANDS OF AN ANGRY GOD"

she, who once was my sister
dead in the house fire
now lying still in the coffin
her hair cut short
by an undertaker who never knew
she called her hair "Wild Ponies"

I don't know any beautiful words
for death or the reason why
sinners curl like blackened leaves
in the hands of God

she, who once was my sister
is now the dust
the soft edge of the earth

SHERMAN ALEXIE (1966–)   241

HAVING A FIGHT WITH YOU

is like being burned up
in a twelfth-floor elevator.
Or drowned in a flipped SUV.

It's like waking with scalpels
arrayed on my chest.
Like being banished to 1983.

Having a fight with you
is never, ever less horrid: that whisper
that says *you never loved me* –

my heart a stalled engine
out the little square window.
Your eyes a white-capped black sea.

242   PATRICK PHILLIPS (1970–)

CONVERSATION BETWEEN
FOX AND FIELD

Fox: Light as
moths, I leave

a trace of
arcs across.

Field: I give
chase until

the brambles,
woods, or fence.

CRANE

The morning almost too white,
I look down and continue peeling plums.
My grandfather dead but not quiet.
The sound of mourning rising and falling,
my grandmother calling all the birds
in Texas by their Ukrainian names,
kran, vorona, shulika.
Our birdhouse overcrowded with
ghosts who push out the hummingbirds
and sing such strange music.

SCHOOL-TO-PRISON PANTS
After Laurie Thomas

They had to be Dickies®, not Dockers®.
They had to include a cellphone pocket
on the right leg, & feign a faint hanging
off our tails in spite of a belt's strangling
support. They had to scream prison, jail,
scream water's rising, scream help-p-p-p
from the lowest floor. But unlike water
they couldn't rise, couldn't obey a warden
lest they risk being jive. They had to be
spread wider than bars. They couldn't be
starched or pressed, but steamed via dryer.
They had to be creaseless, but crisp, khaki
as a waterline staining crest-white Nikes®;
Forces. Lord forbid they be high waters.

LITTLE PRAYER

let ruin end here

let him find honey
where there was once a slaughter

let him enter the lion's cage
& find a field of lilacs

let this be the healing
& if not   let it be

TORSO OF AIR

Suppose you do change your life.
& the body is more than

a portion of night – sealed
with bruises. Suppose you woke

& found your shadow replaced
by a black wolf. The boy, beautiful

& gone. So you take the knife to the wall
instead. You carve & carve

until a coin of light appears
& you get to look in, at last,

on happiness. The eye
staring back from the other side –

waiting.

OCEAN VUONG (1988–)

ACKNOWLEDGMENTS

Thanks are due to the following copyright holders for permission to reprint:

ANNA AKHMATOVA: "The Pillow Hot" translated by D. M. Thomas, from *Selected Poems*, Penguin Books, 1988. FRANCISCO X. ALARCÓN: "A Blank White Page" from *Iguanas in the Snow and Other Winter Poems*. Lee & Low Books, 2001. Reprinted with permission. SHERMAN ALEXIE: "Sinners in the Hands of an Angry God" from *Old Shirts & New Skins*, American Institute Studies Center, University of California, Los Angeles. © 1993 by The Regents of the University of California. MONIZA ALVI: "Rural Scene" from *Split World: Poems 1990–2005*. Bloodaxe Books, 2008. A. R. AMMONS: "Clarifications" and "Salute" from *The Really Short Poems of A. R. Ammons* by A. R. Ammons. Copyright © 1990 by A. R. Ammons. Used by permission of W. W. Norton & Company, Inc. GUILLAUME APOLLINAIRE: "Mirror" translated by Anne Hyde Greet, from *Alcools*. University of California Press, 1965. Reprinted with permission. SIMON ARMITAGE: "Homework" from *The Unaccompanied*. Published by Faber and Faber Limited. Reprinted with permission. "Homework" from *The Unaccompanied: Poems* by Simon Armitage, copyright © 2017 by Simon Armitage. Used by permission of Alfred A. Knopf, an imprint of the Knopf Doubleday Publishing Group, a division of Penguin Random House LLC. All rights reserved. MARGARET ATWOOD: "You Fit Into Me" and "Last Year I Abstained", from *Selected Poems 1965–1975* by Margaret Atwood. Copyright © 1976, renewed 2004 by Margaret Atwood. Used by permission of HarperCollins Publishers. O. W. Toad Ltd c/o Curtis Brown. W. H. AUDEN: "Shorts", copyright © 1974 by The Estate of W. H. Auden; "That Night When Joy Began", copyright 1937 and © renewed 1965 by W. H. Auden; "Epitaph on a Tyrant", copyright 1940 and © renewed 1968 by W. H. Auden; and "August 1968", copyright © 1968 by W. H. Auden; from *Collected Poems* by W. H. Auden, edited by Edward Mendelson. Used by permission of Random House, an imprint and division of Penguin Random House LLC. All rights reserved. "That Night When Joy Began", "August 1968", "Epitaph on a Tyrant", and excerpt from "Shorts" from *Collected Poems*. Curtis Brown Limited. BAI JUYI: "Spring Grasses" translated by Peter Harris, from *Three Hundred Tang Poems* (Everyman's Library, 2009). Reprinted with permission from the translator. MATSUO BASHO:

249